To our Dads, Michael G. Skrobola, Sr. and Irving S. Ziegler, for all their love and support and for being the best Grandpas to our children.

Ashley-Ann listened carefully as her grandpa read to her. She didn't want the story to end.

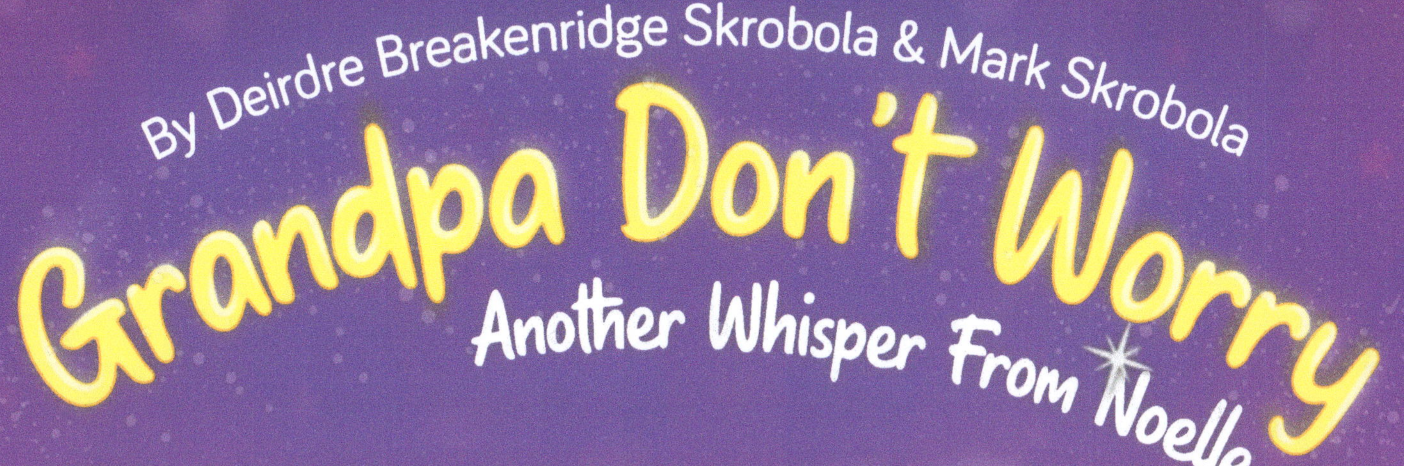

By Deirdre Breakenridge Skrobola & Mark Skrobola
Grandpa Don't Worry
Another Whisper From Noelle
Illustrations by
Daniel Klein

This Whisper belongs to

"And the angel said that they all lived happily ever after."
Grandpa slowly closed the book and kissed
Ashley-Ann on the forehead.

Ashley-Ann looked up at her grandpa and said, "Grandpa, do you believe in angels?"

He smiled and thought for a moment. "Of course I do."

Ashley-Ann was so happy to hear this! She exclaimed, "An angel visited me last night, Grandpa."

It was the second time she'd had a visit from a very special friend.

"An angel named Noelle came to me, and she whispered in my ear."

Her grandpa paused for a moment and said, "What did the angel whisper to you?"

Ashley-Ann looked up at her grandpa and gently put her hand on his face. "Noelle told me to tell you: Grandpa, don't worry."

As Ashley-Ann thought about Noelle's message, she remembered what Noelle wanted her to share with her grandpa. It was a message wrapped in caring, kindness, and love.

"Why did Noelle say this to you?" Ashley-Ann's grandpa was very curious to hear more.

"Grandpa, Noelle said you don't have to worry about family. She said we are strong together and we have good values."

Ashley-Ann wasn't sure she knew what "values" meant. So, she asked Noelle to explain. Noelle mentioned that grandparents and parents teach really important lessons every day.

"Grandpa, Noelle explained to me that values are Loving Lessons. She wanted you to know that through these Loving Lessons, I would grow up to be a good person. I will always help others."

Grandpa smiled and knew Noelle was sharing messages that made him feel happy. He hugged Ashley-Ann and said, "Noelle is really special to visit you, and to share these beautiful messages."

"Oh yes, Grandpa, she is very special, and it's always just a whisper. Her voice is so sweet and soothing. I believe what Noelle says."

"Grandpa, there's something else Noelle really wanted you to know, from now until forever. I remember her words exactly. She wanted me to tell you that I'll be strong in everything I do."

Noelle whispered to Ashley-Ann that someday she would have the strength to take care of herself and others, and she would be strong when people asked her to do things she didn't feel were right.

Ashley-Ann remembered, "Noelle said my strength will help me to always do the right thing."

Grandpa paused for a moment. What Ashley-Ann was sharing suddenly warmed his heart. His love for Ashley-Ann and his family was so important to him. How did Noelle know?

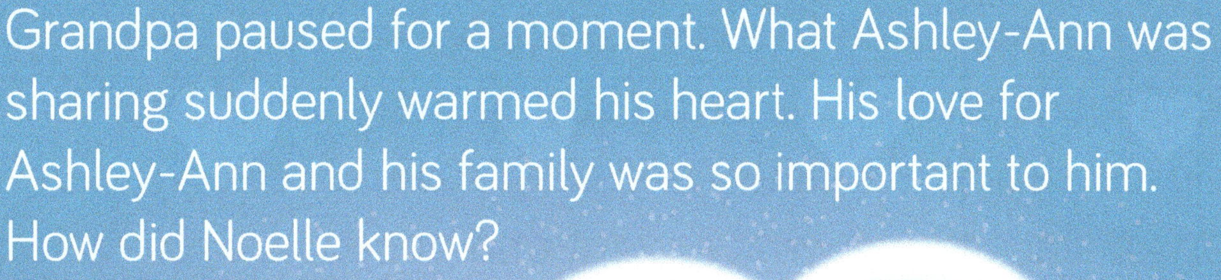

He said to Ashley-Ann, "Everything Noelle has shared with you is true. I want you to be close to your family and to share family values, which are love, kindness, and being good to others."

Grandpa paused and thought carefully. He said to her, "What Noelle said about being strong is also true. I want you to be strong … healthy and strong, which also means always doing what is right and good."

"Oh, Grandpa, I'll be loving, and I'll be healthy and strong," said Ashley-Ann. "Noelle says I will, so you don't have to worry."

"Well then, if Noelle whispered this to you, then I believe her too."

"Grandpa, one last thing Noelle said to me before she left. She said that even though you get worried sometimes, you'll always love me and that makes me feel really happy!"

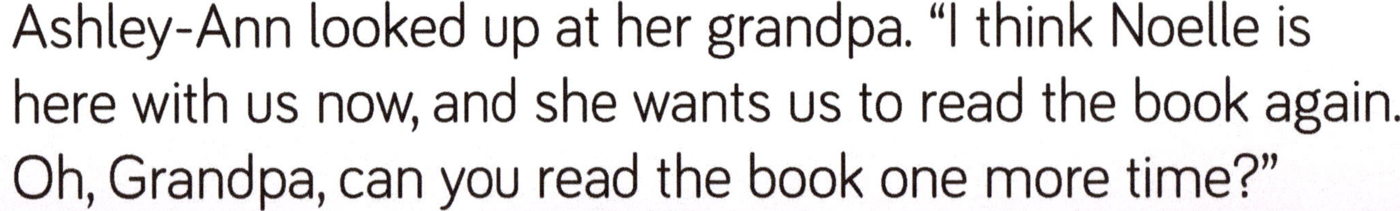

Ashley-Ann looked up at her grandpa. "I think Noelle is here with us now, and she wants us to read the book again. Oh, Grandpa, can you read the book one more time?"

"Okay, just one more time," Grandpa said, smiling.

As Grandpa started the story over, Noelle was there listening,
and she knew her whispers were heard.

The end

FEEL

F = Face your Fears
E = Have Empathy for Others
E = Live with Ethics and Good Judgment
L = Unleash your Love

The Whisper from Noelle Series

See our other books for sale.

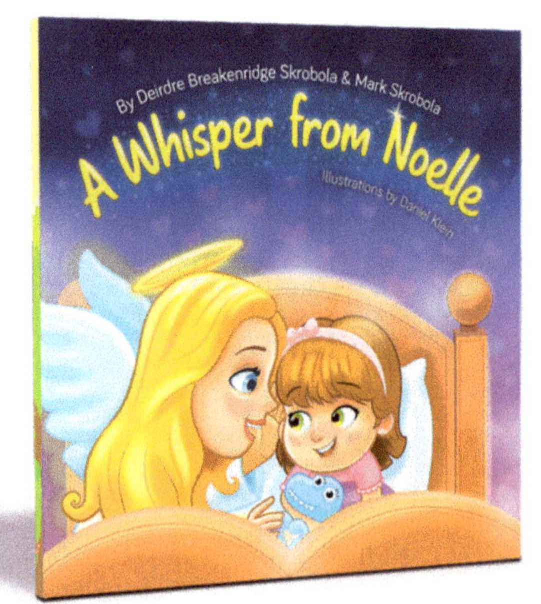

A Whisper From Noelle

One night, Ashley-Ann receives a very special visit while lying in bed. An angel named Noelle comes to her with a series of loving whispers, each with an important message. As Ashley-Ann shares the angel's whispers with her mommy, readers are given the gift of wisdom that Noelle brings to Ashley-Ann. We learn that knowing how to feel will bring kindness, compassion, courage, and the ability to be true to ourselves. This nurturing, insightful story is sure to be a favorite with readers of all ages

Daddy Are You Listening

While walking in the park one day, Ashley-Ann is not sure her daddy listens to her. She shares the week's exciting events, and his mind is elsewhere. Ashley-Ann remembers that her friend, Noelle, an angel, recently visited and whispered an important message in her ear. Noelle told Ashley-Ann that her daddy was trying to listen, and she needed to help him. That day in the park, Ashley-Ann learned how to help her daddy be a better listener and what it means to listen to each other. Children and families can explore feelings and values with this caring message. Listening is the first step to caring, kindness, and showing you understand the ones you love. This insightful story will be a favorite among readers of all ages.

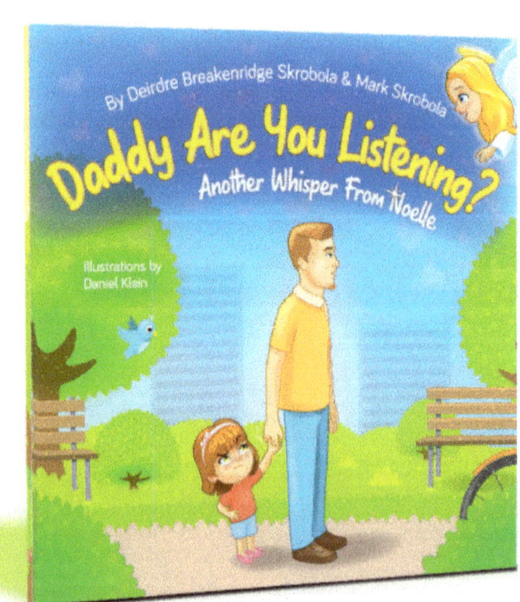